LIFE IN COLONIAL AMERICA

SCHOOLS IN COLONIAL AMERICA

George Capaccio

Cavendish
Square
New York

Published in 2015 by Cavendish Square Publishing, LLC
243 5th Avenue, Suite 136, New York, NY 10016

CPSIA Compliance Information: Batch # WS14CSQ

All websites were available and accurate when this book was sent to press.

Library of Congress Cataloging-in-Publication Data

Capaccio, George.
Schools in colonial America / by George Capaccio.
p. cm. — (Life in colonial America)
Includes index.
ISBN 978-1-62712-894-0 (hardcover) ISBN 978-1-62712-896-4 (ebook)
1. Schools — United States — History — Colonial period, ca. 1600 - 1775 — Juvenile literature. I. Capaccio, George. II. Title.
LA206.C36 2015
370.973—d23

Editorial Director: Dean Miller
Senior Editor: Fletcher Doyle
Copy Editor: Michele Suchomel-Casey
Art Director: Jeffrey Talbot
Designer: Joseph Macri
Production Editor: David McNamara
Production Manager: Jennifer Ryder-Talbot

The photographs in this book are used by permission through the courtesy of: Cover photo by John Greim/age fotostock/SuperStock; North Wind/North Wind Picture Archives, 4; The Bridgeman Art Library/Getty Images, 7; North Wind/North Wind Picture Archives, 8; The Bridgeman Art Library/Getty Images, 10; North Wind Picture Archives/The Image Works, 12; Transcendental Graphics/Archive Photos/Getty Images.,15; Popperfoto/Getty Images, 16; Time Life Pictures/The LIFE Picture Collection/Getty Images, 17; North Wind/North Wind Picture Archives, 18; Hoodinski/File:French and indian war map.svg/Wikimedia Commons, 19; R. E. Collins/File:Nomini Hall Westmoreland County Virginia.jpg/Wikimedia Commons, 20; Library of Congress Prints and Photographs Division, 22; Lawrence Thornton/Archive Photos/Getty Images, 23; North Wind/North Wind Picture Archives, 25; Chronicle/Alamy, 27; North Wind/North Wind Picture Archives, 28; Boston Public Latin School/File:Boston Latin School.JPG/Wikimedia Commons, 31; Sergey Jarochkin/iStock/Thinkstock/Getty Images, 32; North Wind Picture Archives/The Image Works, 34; Mary Evans Picture Library/The Image Works, 35; Jorge Salcedo/Shutterstock.com, 36; Magneticcarpet/File:ClevelandTowerWatercolor20060829.jpg/Wikimedia Commons, 39; Enoch Seeman/File:Elihu Yale by Enoch Seeman the younger 1717.jpeg/Wikimedia Commons, 40; Patrickneil/File:John Carroll statue.jpg/Wikimedia Commons, 42; J. E. Purdy/File:Woodrow Wilson 1902 cph.3b11773.jpg/Wikimedia Commons, 43; MatthewMarcucci/File:PDT and KS.JPG/Wikimedia Commons, 44; Kane5187/File:Eleazar Wheelock.jpg/chipstone.org /Wikimedia Commons, 46; Danita Delimont/Gallo Images/Getty Images, 48; Phrood/File:Hornbooks.png/Wikimedia Commons, 53; MarmadukePercy/File:New-England Primer Enlarged printed and sold by Benjamin Franklin.jpg/Wikimedia Commons, 55; North Wind Picture Archives, 56; Three Lions/Hulton Archive/Getty Images, 58–59; Hulton Archive/Getty Images, 60; DcoetzeeBot/File:Unidentified Artist - Phillis Wheatley - Google Art Project.jpg/Wikimedia Commons, 61; Raymond Gregory/Shutterstock.com, 62; MPI/Archive Photos/Getty Images, 64–65.

Printed in the United States of America

Contents

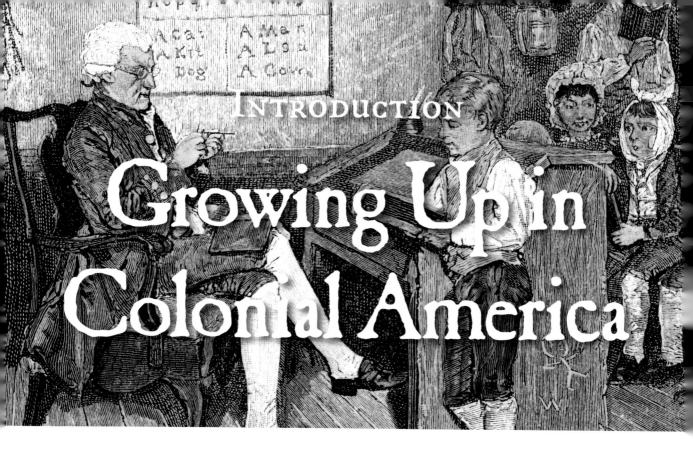

Introduction

Growing Up in Colonial America

n the United States, as in many other countries, children are required by law to obtain an education. Making sure this happens is the responsibility of each state. The age range for compulsory education varies, beginning between five and eight years old and ending between sixteen and eighteen years old, when most students have reached twelfth grade. Children do not have to attend public school in order to fulfill the requirements of the law; they may enroll in a certified private school or take part in an acceptable home-education program. In public and private schools, students are typically divided by age into separate grades.

But things weren't always this way. There was a time when children were not required to attend school. During America's colonial era in the seventeenth and eighteenth centuries, when the original thirteen colonies were under British control, a universal public school system did not exist. The greater part of a child's education took place in the home, where learning to read was the most important educational task. Without this ability, children would have limited access to the Bible, which many believed was the word of God.

In the colonies of New England, where **Puritanism** was the dominant form of Christianity, people saw the world as a constant struggle between the forces of good and evil. The wisdom and moral guidance contained in the Bible offered people protection from the temptations of the devil. In colonial times, education went hand-in-hand with religion. There was no separation, either in the home or in school.

In general, the way colonial children were educated depended on where they lived, the social class to which they belonged, and their gender. In the Puritan North, as previously noted, religious instruction was a major part of a child's education. While Puritans belonged to more than one **Protestant** denomination, in New England most were **Congregationalists**. Members of this group believed that each church, or congregation, should be self-governing and self-sufficient.

The Middle Colonies, by contrast, were much more religiously and culturally diverse. In the Middle Colonies, settlers came from many European countries and belonged to a wide range of Protestant denominations, including Dutch Mennonites, French Huguenots, German Baptists, Lutherans, Anglicans, and **Quakers**. Each denomination established its own type of schooling where students were taught their form of Christianity along with reading, writing, and arithmetic.

In the Southern Colonies, there were fewer schools mainly because people lived in widely separated communities. Children from poor families received only minimal education. Black slaves living and working on plantations typically learned what they needed to serve their white masters. The children of well-to-do farmers were often homeschooled by private tutors (for boys) and **governesses** (for girls). Boys could advance to grammar schools, where they studied Latin and Greek, among other subjects. Grammar schools throughout the colonies prepared students for a college education either in England or in one of the few colleges established in the colonies.

Adolescent boys from wealthy Southern families could plan on becoming a minister, doctor, or other type of professional. But for the most part, their education prepared them to follow in their fathers' footsteps as members of the gentry, who owned and managed large cotton- or tobacco-growing plantations that relied upon slave labor.

Girls in the South learned to read from governesses and were taught the skills they would need as homemakers and Southern wives. In these roles, they would have to supervise their domestic staff and manage household finances, which required competency in arithmetic and record keeping.

Throughout colonial America, the education of girls was not considered important. Since they were expected to marry and have children, girls had to learn how to cook, sew, and knit, among other domestic skills. Knowing how to read was also an essential skill since girls as well as boys were expected to read and study the Bible.

For much of the seventeenth century and well into the eighteenth century, going to school was only a small part of most children's lives. With a growing demand for skilled workers, many boys continued their education as apprentices in the home of a master tradesman or craftsman. In addition to teaching boys a practical trade, masters were also expected to provide religious instruction and basic literacy (reading, writing, and arithmetic). Apprenticeships lasted four to seven years, during which time the apprentice lived with the master's family.

Education in America gradually shifted away from home-based schooling. While parents and guardians remained the primary educators in colonial homes, other institutions began to play a role in children's education. In the chapters that follow, the institutions and the range of educational opportunities available to boys and girls in the colonial era will be closely examined.

Young girls in well-to-do families received instruction in the arts.

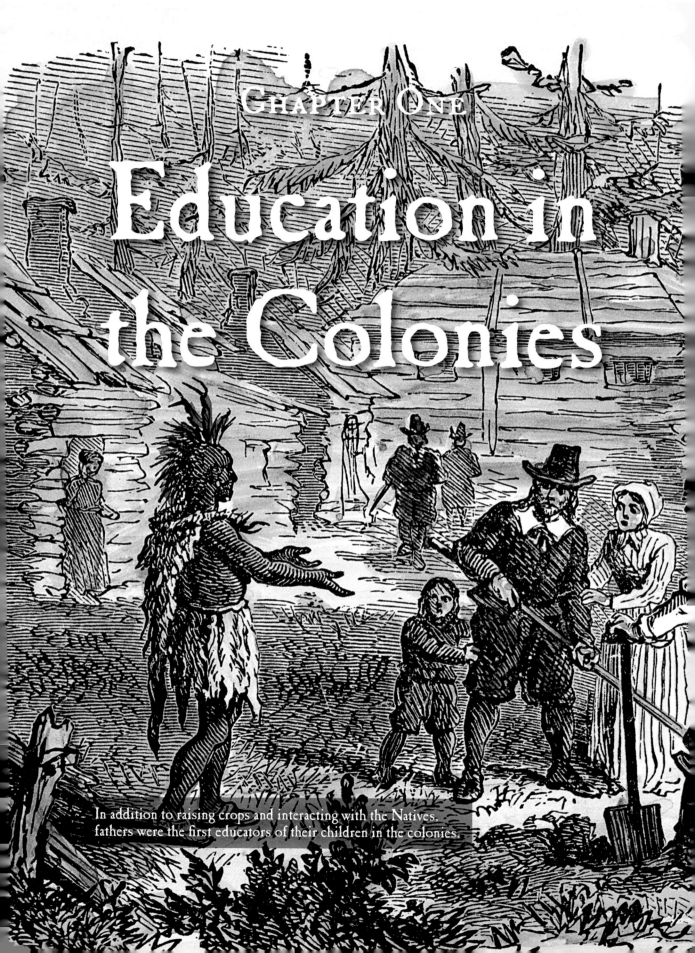

CHAPTER ONE

Education in the Colonies

In addition to raising crops and interacting with the Natives, fathers were the first educators of their children in the colonies.

"We press their memory too soon, and puzzle, strain and load them with words and rules; to know grammar and rhetoric, and a strange tongue or two, that it is ten to one may never be useful to them."
—William Penn, from *Some Fruits of Solitude*, 1693

For most students today, attending school means going to a particular building where students are grouped according to age and grade. Classes typically take place in separate rooms. In secondary schools, there is usually a different teacher for each subject. But for nearly 400 years, from around 1500 to 1900, children growing up in Europe and later in America acquired much of their education at home. Instruction was provided by parents or guardians, or by tutors who came to the home. There was no public school system like the one that exists today in the United States.

The **Pilgrims** who crossed the Atlantic Ocean in 1620 aboard the *Mayflower* established Plymouth Colony, the first English settlement in New England. The Pilgrims included members of a larger religious movement called Puritanism.

These early colonists believed children needed to be able to read the Bible or they would be at risk of leading immoral lives. It was generally assumed that before children attended any sort of school outside of the home, they had to know how to read. In Puritan New England during the seventeenth century, fathers were legally responsible for teaching their children to read. But colonial fathers had another equally important responsibility: to raise their children according to Puritan religious beliefs. To fulfill these related obligations, fathers recited passages from the Bible to their children and had them memorize answers to questions in their **catechism**. At least once a week, children were expected to repeat the answers word for word from memory.

Puritans were expected to be able to read the Bible and read and understand the laws of the land. They believed that in an ideal community members obeyed the laws of man as well as the laws of God, expressed in the Bible and other religious documents. Without understanding both sets of laws, the community would fall into a state of anarchy and sinfulness. In the world of Puritan New England, the ability to read was seen as essential to the survival and advancement of colonial society, and to the salvation of each individual's soul.

The Literacy Law of 1642

In 1630, ten years after English colonists established Plymouth Colony, another group of Puritans left England and sailed to the shores of New England. Under the leadership of John Winthrop, they founded Massachusetts Bay Colony on land that would eventually become the city of Boston. Over the decade of the 1630s, the colony grew as new towns and villages were established.

Massachusetts Bay Colony was the first British American colony to pass laws requiring the education of children. These laws did not demand that children attend school, but they did make education a legal necessity. The first of these laws was passed in 1642. At that time,

Colonial children learned to read with the aid of a hornbook.

Massachusetts had twenty-one towns with a total population of about 9,000. Most towns had a church and a minister with a university education.

Historians consider the 1642 law the first step toward compulsory education in America. It required adults to teach any child in their care to read, and it applied to parents, guardians, and apprenticeship masters. Under this law, children were also expected to understand the moral codes of their religion and the **secular** laws of the colony. Any family that failed to comply with the law could be charged a small fine. The government also claimed the right to remove the child from the home and place him in a setting where he could be properly educated—if his family had not met its obligation.

By 1647, most of the towns in the Massachusetts Bay Colony had failed to provide any kind of public schooling. One reason was the longstanding assumption that learning should take place in the home. For many families, as well as town officials, home schooling was all the education a child needed. Another reason for the lack of public schools was the cost of building and maintaining a school. Some town leaders insisted that there simply wasn't enough money in their town's budget to pay for a school.

THE OLD DELUDER SATAN ACT OF 1647

That same year the Massachusetts General Court passed a second law concerning education. The title of this law was the Old Deluder Satan Act. The Puritans believed that Satan worked hard to prevent people from reading the Bible. The law of 1647 was to be a weapon in the fight against the devil's designs upon humanity.

A related purpose of this law was to overcome parental and government resistance to creating publicly funded schools. This novel piece of legislation required towns with fifty or more homes to hire a schoolmaster. Towns with 100 or more homes had to open a grammar school to prepare boys for college or university studies.

A colonial schoolmaster kept his Bible close by; it played an important role in colonial classrooms.

SCHOOLS IN COLONIAL AMERICA

Many New England families were too poor to send their children to school even in towns with a public school financed by taxpayer money. Families still had to pay a fee toward the schoolmaster's salary. They also had to pay for school supplies, which included quill pens, ink, paper (where it was available), candles, and books. The most expensive item was firewood, which kept the schoolhouse heated. These expenses limited school attendance to families who could afford to pay them.

The Massachusetts Bay Colony led the way in establishing public schools and introducing compulsory education. Other New England Colonies adopted similar literacy laws in the decades that followed: Connecticut in 1650; Plymouth Colony in 1677. But even though these laws existed, enforcing them was a different matter. Many towns just ignored the laws, and many families continued to insist on educating their children at home. For most of the seventeenth century, the Puritan home remained the most important source of a child's education.

Religious Diversity and Parochial Schools

Puritans were the main religious group in New England. In the Middle Atlantic colonies, there was no single religious group that had the same kind of influence over education. Instead, there were many denominations and ethnic groups. Each one established its own private, or **parochial**, school in which children learned a particular form of Christianity in addition to basic literacy. However, this did not apply to Catholics since Catholic education was outlawed for the most part. Catholic parents could only hire Protestant tutors. It wasn't until after the American Revolution that Catholics began to develop their own parochial school system.

The presence of so many different groups, each with its own educational agenda, resulted in fewer public or town schools. Another obstacle to the development of a public school system was the expanse of the Middle Atlantic Colonies. Towns and villages were far apart, and much of the land was wilderness. Providing public schools for a population that was so spread out was a daunting challenge for colonial governments. In addition, many settlers were unwilling to pay taxes to support a public school system.

As in New England, the family home was the place where children began their education. Parents or older siblings taught reading and writing and used instructional materials similar to those in the Northern Colonies: the Bible, catechisms, **hornbooks**, and primers. Children who lived in rural parts of the Middle Atlantic Colonies were often completely dependent on homeschooling. But even in New York and Philadelphia, the largest cities in these colonies, public schools were limited in number.

New York and the Dutch Influence

People from the Netherlands were the first Europeans to settle in what is now New York. They named their colony New Netherlands and established the city of New Amsterdam. (Amsterdam is the capital of the Netherlands.) Dutch schools in colonial America continued the educational practices of schools in the Netherlands. Girls and boys learned reading and writing and some arithmetic. They began their study of reading with a book that included the alphabet, a selection of prayers, a description of religious ceremonies, and the Ten Commandments. The next book in the Dutch curriculum contained passages from the Bible's New Testament. Later books featured the Old Testament, some history, and the catechism of the Dutch Reformed Church, a Protestant Christian denomination.

In 1664, the English took control of New Netherlands and renamed it New York. The city of New Amsterdam became New York City. Throughout the years of British colonial rule, little effort was made in New York to create a public school system. From roughly 1695 to 1775, most children in New York City attended a private school or learned to read and write at home. Many families used religious texts to teach their children.

Private Tutors in New York City

Middle-class parents in New York City tended to regard publicly funded schools as "**charity schools**" for the poor. Because these parents did not want to be thought of as poor, they were reluctant to send their children to these schools. Families with sufficient resources could choose to hire a tutor. But in New York as in the other colonies, qualified tutors were hard to find. Nevertheless, enterprising teachers who hoped to find work as tutors advertised their services in newspapers or put up notices in public places. The following ad by William Elphinston appeared in the *New York Mercury* paper in 1765:

"Teaches persons of both sexes, from 12 years of age and upwards, who never wrote before, to write a good legible hand, in 7 weeks one hour per day, at home or abroad."

Tutors were preferred over public schools by wealthier families in New York City.

Tutors could instruct students in a rented schoolroom or in the homes of the students. Some tutors worked two jobs, teaching children during the day and adults in the evening. In New York City, between 1638 and 1783, tutors outnumbered parochial and town schoolmasters. Their teaching of reading, writing, and arithmetic probably contributed to the rise in literacy during this period. But despite the efforts of tutors, the majority of children in New York City did not attend any school. At most, they received a very modest education at home.

THE QUAKER INFLUENCE

Education in Pennsylvania was different in a variety of ways. The colony was home to a large number of Quakers, who belonged to the Religious Society of Friends.

Quakers believe that all people possess an "Inward Light" or spark of divinity. They are instructed to "walk cheerfully over the world answering that of God in every one," and therefore to treat others as equals worthy of love and respect. The religious ideals of the Quaker faith, when applied to education, gave rise to schools open to all children, regardless of their race, ethnic background, social status, or gender. The Quakers in Pennsylvania even provided free schooling for children whose families were too poor to afford tuition.

The founder and governor of Pennsylvania was William Penn, an English Quaker. Despite Penn's commitment to education, the colonial government was reluctant to offer financial support for Quaker schools, which had to rely on donations, tuition, and other sources.

William Penn advocated a basic education for all children.

Quakers weren't interested in developing a college-educated ministry and believed that too much education was not in the best interest of children. Instead, they advocated basic literacy combined with learning a trade.

Many other Pennsylvania parents wanted their children to attend a Latin grammar school, so they hired educated tutors from England who could teach boys Latin, Greek, and arithmetic. These subjects prepared students for grammar schools, which were a stepping-stone to a college or university education.

PROMOTING LITERACY

In addition to Quakers, other religious denominations worked to advance literacy in Pennsylvania. The Anglican Church launched a major **missionary** effort in 1701. Support from the British government allowed Anglican ministers and teachers in America to provide children with religion-based literacy programs. The organization directly responsible for setting up and funding these programs was the Anglican Society for the Propagation of the Gospel in Foreign Parts, otherwise known as the SPG.

Teachers employed by the SPG taught classes anywhere that was convenient for students. Education included basic literacy and religious instruction and was available to boys and girls as well as young men and women. SPG schools welcomed African Americans and Native Americans and members of the Anglican Church, as well as those who challenged its teachings.

In rural Pennsylvania, SPG schoolmasters taught basic literacy in the summer to children who couldn't attend school during spring planting or the

John Woolman, a Quaker born in New Jersey in 1720, worked hard for the just treatment of Native Americans.

fall harvest. They also provided evening classes for **indentured** servants, apprentices, and other workers who were unable to attend school during the day. Education began with learning to read. Next, students learned writing and arithmetic. The formal schooling of girls didn't advance much beyond literacy, religious instruction, and learning domestic skills. But boys who completed their schooling could learn a trade by entering an apprenticeship.

Evert Pietersen traveled to farms to teach children in their homes.

Like the Quakers and the Anglicans, members of the Lutheran, German Reformed, and Scots-Irish Presbyterian churches established schools in many parts of Pennsylvania. Before William Penn became the colony's first governor, Dutch and Swedish immigrants had established their own settlements. Their ministers often served as roving schoolmasters. One such teacher, Evert Pietersen, taught school to twenty-five children who lived in separate villages. Instead of having them travel to a schoolhouse, he went to them, one family at a time. In 1657, he described his work: "For families living far from churches, ministers and their assistants, [I] visited families as far as practical, and in conjunction with parents, [I] taught the young what they could, at least to read and write and recite Bible lessons and the catechism."

Despite these varied efforts, the level of literacy in Pennsylvania remained low. This was especially true outside of Philadelphia, one of colonial America's largest and most important cities. Attempts to start a public school system paid for with taxpayer money never made much progress. One of the reasons was the large number of religious and ethnic groups. Trying to bring these diverse groups to some sort of agreement concerning education was not easy.

Another obstacle to improving literacy among the colony's children included ongoing warfare between Great Britain and France. These conflicts endangered many colonial families in Pennsylvania and made the pursuit of education secondary to the need for survival. To pay for the war, Great Britain demanded higher taxes from British colonials in North America, and higher taxes meant less money available for education. Compared to other colonies,

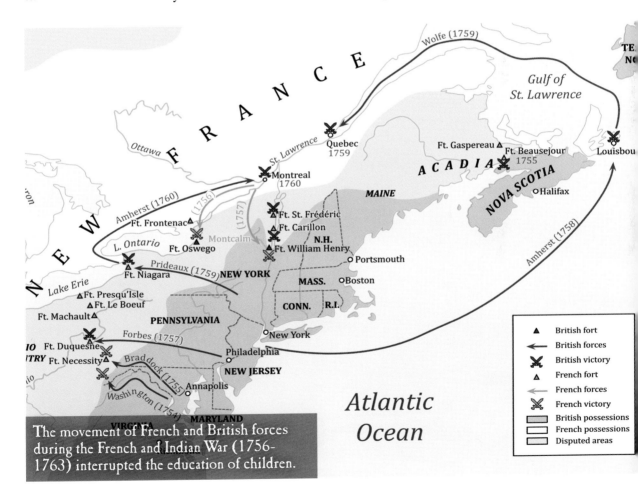

The movement of French and British forces during the French and Indian War (1756-1763) interrupted the education of children.

Pennsylvania lagged behind in terms of its commitment to literacy. By the time of the American Revolution in 1775, many children and adults in Pennsylvania had received only minimal schooling.

Tutors and Old Field Schools

In the 1770s, a well-educated young man named Philip Vickers Fithian worked as a private tutor in the home of Colonel and Mrs. Robert Carter. The Carter family lived in the colony of Virginia. They owned a large plantation and belonged to the Southern **aristocracy**, or upper class. Like other members of this class, they hired tutors to educate their children.

Fithian had graduated with a degree in **theology** from Princeton College in New Jersey. His studies had prepared him to become a minister, but before beginning his career, he tried his hand at tutoring. His students included the Carters' two sons, five daughters, and a nephew. The children ranged in age from five to seventeen. This excerpt from the *Journal and Letters of Philip Vickers Fithian* gives a glimpse of Fithian's life as a tutor in the colonial South:

Nomini Hall was the name of the plantation owned by the Carter family, who hired a tutor for their children.

"In the morning so soon as it is light a Boy knocks at my Door to make a fire; after the Fire is kindled, I rise which now in the winter is commonly by Seven, or a little after. By the time I am [dressed] the Children commonly enter the School-Room, which is under the Room I sleep in; I hear them round one lesson, when the Bell rings for eight o-Clock . . . the Children then go out; and at half after eight the Bell rings for Breakfast, we then repair to the Dining-Room; after Breakfast, which is generally about half after nine, we go into School, and sit til twelve, when the Bell rings, & they go out for noon; the dinner-Bell rings commonly about half after two, often at three, but never before two—After dinner is over, which is common, when we have no Company, is about half after three we go into School, & sit till the Bell rings at five, when they separate til the next morning . . ."

Fithian taught Mr. and Mrs. Carter's daughters reading, writing, and some arithmetic. Other tutors came to the plantation to give the girls dancing, singing, and music lessons. The boys received a more comprehensive education that included Greek and Latin grammar and literature. The younger boys and girls also studied their catechism with Fithian. Except for the catechism lesson, which was probably a group activity, Fithian provided one-on-one instruction and customized his curriculum to match the abilities and needs of his students.

Fithian's schoolhouse was one of several buildings on the Carter plantation. Records show that it was 45 feet (13.7 meters) long by 27 feet (8.2 m) wide and made of bricks. The schoolhouse had five rooms and two floors. Fithian's living quarters were on the second floor. His classroom was on the ground floor along with two other rooms. Each of the five rooms had its own fireplace. The building was similar in size and construction to schoolhouses on other Southern plantations during the colonial period.

Not all schoolmasters in Virginia or the other Southern Colonies enjoyed such a comfortable environment. Small farmers and planters sometimes combined their resources and opened up an "**old field school**." The site was usually farmland that was no longer in use. The schoolhouse might be an abandoned

Unused buildings in the South were often turned into field schools.

tobacco shed, an old barn, or a one-room building. A local schoolmaster, hired by neighboring farmers, would teach reading and writing but not much else.

John Davis, an Englishman born in 1776, came to America in search of tutoring opportunities. He taught the children of a Quaker family in Virginia for a few months and then went to work for a nearby planter. His students included the planter's daughter as well as children from the neighborhood. The school—a log house—was an old field school. The first day of class showed Davis how much the local farmers valued the services he could provide:

"The following day every farmer came from the neighborhood to the house, who had any children to send to my Academy, for such they did me the honour to term the log-hut in which I was to teach. Each man brought his son, or his daughter, and rejoiced that the day was arrived when their little ones could light their tapers at the torch of knowledge! I was confounded at the [praise] they heaped upon a man whom they had never seen before . . . No price was too great for the services I was to render their children . . ."

The Education of George Washington

It's hard to generalize about educational patterns, especially in an area as large and diverse as the Southern Colonies of British America. For example, some old field schools provided a quality education. George Washington, the first president of the United States, attended such a school. He began his formal education at home with a tutor from England. Later, he went to an old field school where the local **sexton**, or church caretaker, also worked as a teacher. For another year, Washington rode on horseback to a different field school about 10 miles (16 kilometers) from his home. Then he attended a third school in Fredericksburg, Virginia. To get there, Washington had to row each morning and night across the Rappahannock River. When he was thirteen, Washington finished his formal education, which it inspired him to undertake self-learning.

George Washington lived in this house at Ferry Farm in Fredericksburg, Virginia, as a boy, and went to school in a small house on the property.

George Washington was schooled similar to the way other early American leaders obtained theirs in the colonial South. Like Washington, Thomas Jefferson and James Madison, two of the country's Founding Fathers and future presidents, were taught by private tutors and local schoolmasters. Thomas Jefferson started his education at the age of five when he and other children went to school in a small house on the family plantation. James Madison learned to read and write at home thanks to the efforts of his mother and grandmother. Then he attended a boarding school where a Scottish schoolmaster taught him Latin, Greek, geography, algebra, geometry, and literature.

CIVIL BEHAVIOR

When George Washington was around sixteen, his schoolmaster gave him a lesson in penmanship. George had to copy a list of 110 rules from *Rules of Civility & Decent Behaviour In Company and Conversation*, a book by French clerics written in 1595. Here is a short list of these rules (George's spelling and punctuation have not been changed from his original exercise book):

1st Every Action done in Company, ought to be with Some Sign of Respect, to those that are Present.

2nd When in Company, put not your Hands to any Part of the Body, not usualy Discovered.

3rd Shew Nothing to your Freind that may affright him.

4th In the Presence of Others Sing not to yourself with a humming Noise, nor Drum with your Fingers or Feet.

Apprenticeships for the Poor

During the colonial period, many Southerners insisted that the home was the proper place for schooling and that education should be the responsibility of the family. They did not favor using taxpayer money to support public schools for the general population. In Virginia, however, the government assumed some responsibility for educating orphans, poor children, or children from homes where the parents failed to provide even basic literacy. But a more common way to provide schooling for disadvantaged children was through the apprenticeship system. Upon reaching a certain age, such children could be sent to live with a master tradesman. The contract between the master and the child's family or guardian typically included a clause that legally bound the master to teach the child reading and writing in addition to the trade itself.

A colonial blacksmith and his two apprentices take a break from their difficult labor.

EDUCATION FOR THE CHILDREN OF PROSPEROUS SOUTHERN FAMILIES

Southern society had two very distinct classes—the rich and the poor. It would take many years before a thriving middle class emerged. Educational practices in many ways preserved the class structure of the South. Children born into wealthy families had the benefit of home tutors, often from England or the Northern colonies. Boys who completed their initial schooling were sent to prestigious colleges in the North or to universities in England. They might pursue a career in law or medicine or return home to help their fathers manage the family plantation.

Southern girls from well-to-do families were rarely encouraged to pursue their education beyond basic literacy and domestic skills. Under the guiding hand of a governess (a female tutor), they might study a foreign language (usually French) as well as dancing, music, social **etiquette**, weaving, cooking, and nursing.

In general, educational opportunities in the South depended on where people lived and to which economic class they belonged. Wealthy families employed private tutors and sent their sons to England or colleges in the North to further their education. Smaller farmers would often start an old field school on an acre or two of **fallow** land and hired a local schoolmaster to teach reading and writing to neighborhood children.

Apprenticeships were available for orphans and children from poor families as a way for them to learn how to read and write. Another route to literacy was through religion. Different Christian denominations established their own parochial schools for children in the South. One of the most influential of these religious groups was the Anglican Church and its Society for the Propagation of the Gospel (SPG). As it had done in the Middle Atlantic Colonies, the SPG started several charity schools in the early 1700s. It was also one of the first groups to create schools specifically for the children of African American slaves.

CHILDREN'S PICTURE ROLL

THE SWAN

A governess in the home of a Southern colonial family gives her young pupils a reading lesson.

CHAPTER TWO
Types of Schooling

In many colonial homes, parents and grandparents served as teachers for the family's children.

"Thinking my apprenticeship very tedious, I was continuously
wishing for some opportunity of shortening it,"
—Ben Franklin, on his time learning the printing trade
from his brother, James

Children growing up in the British American colonies had a variety of ways to become educated, even in places without a publicly funded school system. Parents, other elders, or older siblings often assumed responsibility for teaching children how to read. In some homes, a tutor or governess would provide the reading instruction. Outside of the home, institutions developed to meet the educational needs of colonial children.

DAME SCHOOLS

Women in a town or village who needed extra income could offer schooling and child care for the children of neighborhood families. These women were known as "dames," and the home-based schools they opened were called dame schools. They were also known as petty schools. The word "petty" probably comes from the French word *petit* (pe-TEE), which means small. For a fee, parents could drop off their boys and girls at the home of a local "dame," who would give lessons in reading and simple arithmetic. She would also help the children develop basic social skills much as today's preschool and kindergarten teachers attempt to do. The quality of instruction in a dame school depended on the abilities of the teacher and her level of education.

A day at a dame school was not all discipline and hard work. The woman who ran the school could alternate between doing her household chores and instructing the children. Usually, there weren't more than fifteen students in a dame school class, and there could be as few as three. The children were expected to stay out of mischief and practice good manners.

The dame school teacher used simple religious texts to help her students master the alphabet and learn to spell. She taught girls sewing and knitting and introduced boys to writing, which in those days meant good penmanship.

Not all dame schools were private ventures. Some were partly paid for by the town and therefore qualified as semipublic schools. As dame schools became more public, towns began paying dame school teachers a small salary so they didn't have to rely on tuition paid by students' parents. As salaries increased, towns assumed greater control of these schools. By 1789, Massachusetts required all dame school teachers to obtain a teaching license.

An important stage in education, dame schools prepared children to enter town schools, which were either grammar schools that taught grammar, reading, and writing, or writing schools that taught only writing.

LATIN GRAMMAR SCHOOLS

Latin grammar schools were comparable to our high schools. Their main purpose was to prepare students for higher learning at a college or university. But in colonial times, enrollment in a Latin grammar school was usually limited to boys. On top of gender bias, there was also a bias in favor of boys from upper-class families. Prominent, well-educated members of this class who sent their sons to Latin grammar schools expected them to undertake a professional career instead of learning a trade.

The building in the foreground is Boston Latin. Founded in 1635, it was the first public school in the United States.

The first Latin grammar school was founded in 1635 in Boston, Massachusetts. Unlike most schools of this type, it was a free grammar school open to boys from any social class. Initially modeled after the English grammar school, it provided a solid, seven-year education in Greek and Latin, among other classical subjects. In 1877, the Girls' Latin School opened, and in 1972, Boston Latin taught both sexes. This school represented the beginning of America's public school system. Still going strong, Boston Latin is the country's oldest existing school.

QUILL PENS

The invention of fountain pens in the 1880s ended more than 1,000 years of reliance on quill pens. The word "pen" comes from the Latin word penna, which means feather. Quill pens were made from the wing feathers of certain birds, mainly geese, turkeys, swans, or crows. Thomas Jefferson, America's third president, raised his own flock of geese to make sure he always had a ready supply of goose feathers for his writing.

Transforming the wing feather of a goose or other type of bird into a pen was no easy task. There are at least ten steps involved just in preparing and carving the shaft of the pen and almost as many steps in making the nib, which is the pointed tip of the pen.

A quill pen tended to last about a week. Some of the world's most treasured documents—including the Declaration of Independence, the poems of William Shakespeare, and the U.S. Constitution—were written with quill pens.

Only boys who had achieved proficiency in reading and writing could hope to be admitted to a Latin grammar school. During their years in grammar school, they would study Greek and Latin and the literature written in these two languages. Without a strong foundation in Greek and Latin, they would have little chance of passing the college or university entrance exam. The grammar school curriculum also included higher mathematics.

The absence of a government-supported public school system meant that the education of poor children was often neglected—unless they happened to find support from a private citizen.

APPRENTICESHIPS

"'Open the door!' 'I will not open it.' 'Wherefore not?' 'The knife is in the meat, and the drink is in the horn, and there is revelry in Arthur's Hall; and none may enter therein but the son of a King of a privileged country, *or a craftsman bringing his craft*.'"

—from *The Red Book of Hergest*, a 14th century Welsh manuscript

This scrap of dialogue from a **medieval** book of poems and prose illustrates the respect that craft workers commanded in England many centuries ago. Craft workers who immigrated to America in the seventeenth and eighteenth centuries enjoyed a similar respect. They also carried on the age-old master-apprentice relationship in order to pass their skills to the next generation.

In most of the colonies, apprenticeship training was a common way for children to acquire a basic education in literacy. A second, equally important benefit was learning a trade or craft that would enable a young man to start a business. As a skilled worker, he had a better chance of earning enough to support a family and remain financially independent.

As the population in the colonies grew, so too did the need for skilled workers. After a child had completed an elementary education at a dame school, his family might enroll him in a grammar school or arrange for him to become an apprentice. Since most boys weren't going to college, there was no reason for

Types of Schooling

them to attend a grammar school. An apprenticeship was a practical alternative.

The apprenticeship system in New England had the backing of the law. Apprenticeship laws required the master tradesman or craftsman to continue the literacy training of his young apprentice while teaching him the skills he would need in his particular field. The laws also required the master to support his apprentice by providing food and shelter and other necessities. There was nothing in the laws about compulsory school attendance. However, the master was legally obliged to make sure his apprentice learned to read.

Contracts between the child's family and the master were signed. The courts had the power to enforce the terms if either party failed to meet them. Apprenticeships usually began when the child was around eight or nine and lasted until the age of twenty-one for boys and eighteen for girls. Massachusetts in 1710 amended its apprenticeship laws to require boys to learn both reading and writing and girls to learn only reading.

Masters, such as these in a colonial era print shop, were required to teach their apprentices how to read.

Male apprentices learned a range of skills, from blacksmithing to tailoring. But female apprentices were only expected to learn "women's work" or "house-wifery." According to the Puritan view, writing (actually, penmanship) was not something women needed to know in order to be competent homemakers. Men, on the other hand, were preparing for employment as skilled workers. For them, writing was an essential skill.

The home of the English-born Anne Bradstreet in North Andover, Massachusetts.

America's First Women Poet

Anne Bradstreet (born Anne Dudley) never went to school. Yet she is regarded as one of the finest women poets in British America and the first woman poet to be published both in England and the New World. Born into a cultured Puritan family in England, Anne was schooled at home. Private tutors, in addition to Anne's educated father, gave her lessons in history, literature, and several languages. When she was sixteen, she married Simon Bradstreet, who was nine years older. In 1630, she, Simon, and her parents emigrated.

Even with Anne's chronic health problems, she and her husband made a home for themselves and raised eight children in New England. She continued her pursuit of knowledge despite the widely held Puritan belief that too much learning would harm a woman's "feminine nature." Though she experienced many difficult periods, her religious faith and the love she felt for her family gave her the strength to keep going.

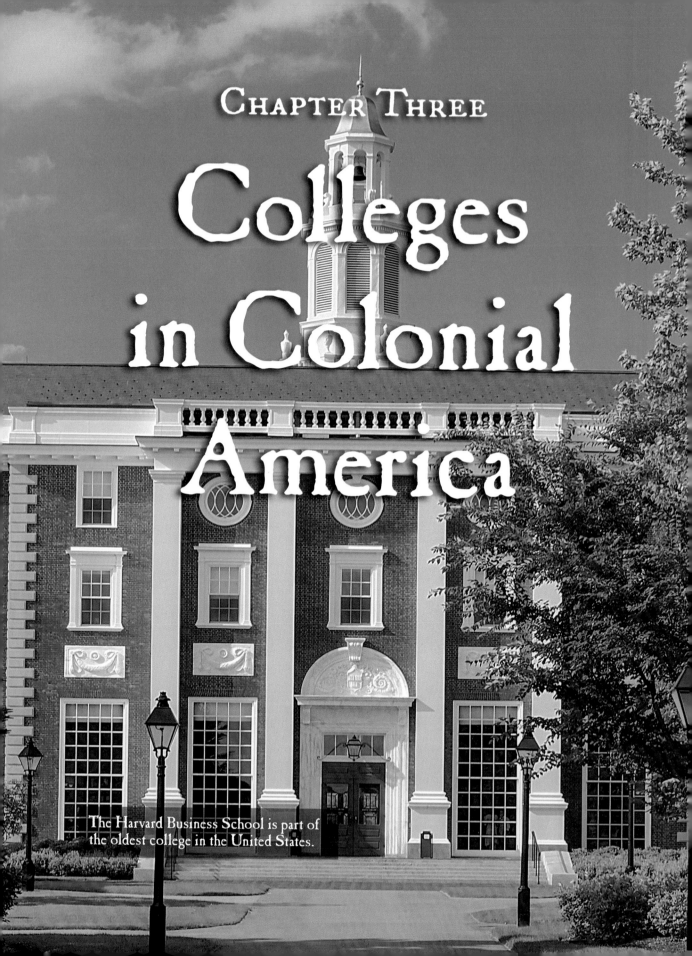

CHAPTER THREE

Colleges in Colonial America

The Harvard Business School is part of the oldest college in the United States.

"That none may Expect to be admitted into this College unless upon Examination of the Praesident and Tutors, They shall be found able Extempore to Read, Construe and Parse Tully, Virgil and the Greek Testament: and to write True Latin Prose and to understand the Rules of Prosodia, and Common Arithmetic, and shall bring Sufficient Testimony of his Blameless and inoffensive Life."
—Regulations at Yale College, 1745

The influence of religion remained strong through much of the colonial era and played an important part in the development of colleges. By the time of the American Revolution in 1775, there were nine colleges in the colonies, and most of them were affiliated with a particular Protestant denomination. For example, Harvard College in Massachusetts strongly reflected the faith and ideals of its Puritan founders. The College of New Jersey (later renamed Princeton University) owes its founding to the Presbyterians.

American colleges were modeled after England's two oldest universities—Oxford and Cambridge. Like their English models, American colleges prepared young men for careers in law, medicine, religion (as members of the clergy), and other professions. As in England, acceptance was limited to white, Christian males whose families were wealthy enough to afford the high cost of tuition. Colonial laws as well as long-standing traditions forbade women and African Americans from attending college. In the case of Native

Americans, colleges defended their exclusiveness by claiming that graduates could serve as missionaries. Drawing upon their training and education, these young men would have the necessary resources to convert Native Americans to Christianity.

The British government, through much of the colonial period, was not interested in supporting the growth of colleges. Its main interest was trade: The colonies were intended to serve as markets for British goods and as a source of raw materials for British factories. In the eyes of British merchants and members of the ruling class, a college education was not likely to increase the flow of profits to the homeland. But despite the British Empire's lack of support for colonial colleges, these institutions managed to gain a foothold in America.

Many colonists tended to view a college education as unnecessary to a successful life. The sons of wealthy planters and businessmen, for instance, could look forward to professional success without the benefit of a college education. During colonial times, experience and character carried much more value than a diploma from an accredited college. In fact, some of the people who played a leading role in the American Revolution—men like George Washington and Benjamin Franklin—never went to college yet still managed to achieve remarkable success in their chosen fields.

On the other hand, thanks in large part to their education, graduates of America's colonial colleges were among the fledgling country's greatest political and religious leaders. The men who envisioned and designed a revolutionary form of government owed much of their intellectual prowess to what they learned in college.

The College Try

In seventeenth-century New England, Puritans wanted to make sure their churches would always have a ready supply of ministers. To this end, the Puritans established the first college in British America—Harvard College.

Founded in 1626, Harvard began with nine students and one schoolmaster. It was named after John Harvard, a young minister who died in 1638, leaving

The Cleveland Tower was built as a memorial to President Grover Cleveland at Princeton University, which began as the College of New Jersey.

A gift from businessman Elihu Yale allowed a new school to be built in New Haven, Connecticut.

half his estate to the college. A statue of this generous patron can be seen in Harvard Yard in Cambridge, Massachusetts.

In 1693, the reigning monarchs of Britain—Queen Mary II and King William III—signed a royal **charter** that authorized the establishment of the College of William and Mary in the Virginia Colony. Plans for this college were under way several years before the founding of Harvard College in 1626. But because of conflict with local Native Americans, construction didn't begin until 1695.

After Harvard, the College of William and Mary is the second oldest college in America and has the distinction of being the "Alma Mater of a Nation" since some of the country's Founding Fathers attended this school. George Washington at age seventeen obtained his surveyor's license through the college, and presidents Thomas Jefferson and James Monroe received their undergraduate education here. Washington would eventually become the school's first American chancellor, or president.

The College of William and Mary was the first American college to gain university status. It is also the first law school in America and the first school to introduce a student honor code governing behavior. In 1918, it opened its doors to women students.

The history of Yale University begins in the 1640s, when a group of colonial clergymen set out to build a college in New Haven, Connecticut. Their dream didn't become a reality until 1701 with the founding of the Collegiate School of Saybrook, "wherein Youth may be instructed in the Arts and Sciences [and] through the blessing of Almighty God may be fitted for Publick employment both in Church and Civil State."

In 1718, Elihu Yale, a successful merchant and **philanthropist**, donated his collection of books, a portrait of King George I, and a variety of imported textiles to the school. Yale's gifts were sold in Boston, and the money was used to build a new school in New Haven, Connecticut. In honor of Elihu Yale and his generous **endowment**, the new school was named Yale College. In 1745 Yale College became Yale University.

Father John Carroll, who founded Georgetown University in 1789, was the first Roman Catholic bishop in the United States.

Start of an Era

America's colonial colleges all began with strong ties to Protestant denominations. Georgetown University, however, has a different story to tell. Founded in 1789, when the colonial era was over and freedom of religion was written into the Constitution, Georgetown is the oldest Catholic university in the United States. Located in the nation's capital, it overlooks the Potomac River. Since the first classes were held in 1792, the school has become an internationally recognized academic and research institution.

During its first year, more than forty students were enrolled. Attendance gradually increased until the Civil War (1861–1865) when most of the students left school to fight on one side or the other. When the war ended, students chose gray and blue as their school colors: blue for the Union side and gray for the Confederate side.

The next year, New Jersey granted a charter to the College of New Jersey. Unlike other colonial charters, this one permitted "any Person of any religious Denomination whatsoever" to attend. Despite having a charter, the college's initial enrollment amounted to ten students who met for classes in a clergyman's living room in Elizabeth, New Jersey.

Ten years later, the college moved to Nassau Hall in Princeton, New Jersey. At the time of its construction, Nassau Hall was one of the biggest buildings in the colonies, and it served as a design model for other college buildings such as Harvard's Hollis Hall.

Woodrow Wilson, the thirteenth president of Princeton University, was the twenty-eighth president of the United States.

During the American Revolution, Nassau Hall was occupied at various times by soldiers from both sides. Until the nineteenth century, the building sheltered all of the college's facilities—dormitories, classrooms, library, chapel, dining room, and kitchen. In 1896, the College of New Jersey acquired the name it bears today—Princeton University. One of the university's most prominent alumni is Woodrow Wilson, who graduated with a baccalaureate degree in 1879. Later in his career, he became the thirteenth president of Princeton and in 1912, the twenty-eighth president of the United States. Under Wilson's leadership (1902–1910), Princeton grew dramatically. He added a graduate school and doubled the size of the faculty.

CAUGHT IN CONFLICT

King George II of England granted a royal charter in 1754 to King's College in the colony of New York. Its location and religious character were points of contention between various groups. Those who wanted New York City to be the home of King's College got their way, while Anglicans won the vote for religious affiliation.

A schoolhouse built beside Trinity Church in what is now lower Manhattan served as the first home for the new college. The first classes had eight students. But over the next few decades, enrollment steadily grew as did the size and reputation of King's College. The American Revolution halted all instruction for eight years. In 1784, it reopened but with a different name—Columbia. Though it continued to reflect its Anglican roots, Columbia University established a much more diverse community of teachers and students.

The Phi Delta Theta fraternity house is part of the University of Pennsylvania, which was founded by Ben Franklin.

The University of Pennsylvania owes its existence to the vision and hard work of Benjamin Franklin, a citizen of Philadelphia. Franklin started as a printer's apprentice working for his older brother James. But over the course of his long life, Franklin gained fame as an inventor, a scientist, and a staunch advocate for American independence. Along with Thomas Jefferson and three others, Franklin helped to draft the Declaration of Independence on the eve of the American Revolution.

Before becoming active in politics, Franklin devoted his talent and energy to improving life for his fellow citizens. One of the many projects he undertook was the creation of a college he named "the Publick Academy of Philadelphia." With his characteristic flair for innovation, he envisioned a school that would teach students practical skills—in addition to the standard curriculum. This was a unique departure from the mainly religious education other colonial colleges provided.

In 1751, Franklin's academy finally became a reality. Later, during the years of the Revolution, the state of Pennsylvania seized control of the college and turned it into the University of the State of Pennsylvania. Its **nonsectarian** faculty was the first of its kind in the newly formed United States, while its **board of trustees** represented not one but many Christian denominations. In 1791, the university became a private institution once more and changed its name to the University of Pennsylvania.

Brown, established in 1764, was New England's third colonial college and one of the first to accept students without regard for their religious beliefs. Originally called the College of Rhode Island, Brown moved from Warren to Providence in 1770. The school was renamed Brown in 1804 in honor of Nicholas Brown, a Providence businessman who donated $5,000, a substantial amount in those days. In 1891 Brown began admitting women to its Women's College, later called Pembroke College in Brown University.

Rutgers was called Queen's College when it was chartered in 1766, but it soon found itself caught up in the American war for independence. Once the fighting began, churches and private homes served as temporary classrooms.

After the war, financial problems forced Queen's College to shut down and reopen on two occasions between 1795 and 1825. During its second reopening, the school changed its name to Rutgers in recognition of Colonel Henry Rutgers, who fought in the American Revolution.

FULFILLMENT OF A DREAM

Dartmouth College, located in Hanover, New Hampshire, can trace its history back to the efforts of Reverend Eleazar Wheelock (1711–1779), a Connecticut minister and educator. In the 1730s, Wheelock started a Latin grammar school to prepare young boys for college.

Reverend Eleazar Wheelock founded Dartmouth College and established the Indian Charity School for Native Americans.

FIRST PUPIL WAS A MOHEGAN

One of the most famous students at Reverend Eleazar Wheelock's Latin grammar school was Samson Occom, a Mohegan Indian. When he was twenty years old, Occom enrolled. The minister's deep concern for the plight of Native Americans and his association with Occom, who became a Presbyterian minister, inspired him to start a charity school for indigenous children. Funded through donations, the school would provide secular and religious education and prepare boys to serve their people as Christian missionaries.

In the 1750s, he opened a charity school for the education of Native American boys and operated it along with his Latin Grammar School. He wanted to add a college but couldn't get a charter from Connecticut, so Revered Wheelock was forced to search for a new location. In 1769 he succeeded in winning a charter from King George III, thanks to support from the royal governor of New Hampshire. The college would educate white students in traditional subjects such as philosophy and literature. He named the college Dartmouth after William Legge, the Earl of Dartmouth in England.

In 1770, the first class was held in a log cabin in Hanover. Just four students were present. From this unlikely start, Dartmouth College has grown into a major institution of higher learning. In 1972 it became coeducational. That same year, Dartmouth set up a Native American program, one of the first in the country.

CHAPTER FOUR

The Colonial Classroom

One-room schools were common in many rural and small towns. A single teacher was tasked to educate several grade levels of elementary-age students.

*"A knowledge of books is the basis upon
which other knowledge is to be built."*
—George Washington, to Jonathan Boucher, July 9, 1771

In colonial America, "school" didn't necessarily refer to a specific setting. A school could be just about anywhere children and teachers were gathered—in town churches and meetinghouses, shops, barns, even inns and taverns.

Moreover, the definition of "teacher" was as variable as the definition of school. A teacher could be a schoolmaster, a parent, an older brother or sister, a shopkeeper, or a master craftsman.

Many people felt strongly that the home was the preferred environment for teaching children the basics, especially in the first decades of the seventeenth century. But over time, institutions outside of the home gradually took on more and more of the responsibility for educating children. One of these institutions was the one-room schoolhouse. Small colonial communities lacked the resources to build elaborate structures. One-room schoolhouses were typically around 20 feet (6 m) long and 18 feet (5.4 m) wide with a six- or seven-foot (1.8–2.1 m) ceiling and two or three windows. Walls were coated with lime plaster, a whitish material that brightened the room. On dark afternoons, candles or whale oil lamps added extra light.

The children sat on three-legged stools or on long, backless planks made from pine or oak. For desks, they had similar long planks. A fireplace or potbellied stove provided heat. To pay for part of their children's education, parents often sent them to school with wood for the fireplace. In some schools, children who failed to bring their share of firewood were punished by having to sit in the coldest part of the room.

Students sitting too far from the fireplace or the stove during the winter had to wear many layers of clothing to keep warm. But sitting too close had its own drawback since the heat could easily cause even the most focused young learner to become drowsy and even fall asleep.

A New England Schoolhouse

In 1833, Warren Burton, a native New Englander, published *The District School As It Was*, a book about the one-room schoolhouse he attended. The school he describes was typical of early New England schools:

"The fire-place was on the right, half way between the door of entrance and another leading into a dark closet, where the girls put their outside garments and their dinner baskets. This also served as a fearful dungeon for the [enclosing] of offenders. Directly opposite the fire-place was an aisle, two feet and a half wide, running up an inclined floor to the opposite side of the room . . . Every cold forenoon, the old fire-place, wide and deep, was kept a roaring furnace of flame, for the benefit of blue noses, chattering jaws and aching toes, in the more distant regions."

Schoolmasters had only the most basic teaching tools, usually a few books and sometimes an **abacus** for teaching arithmetic. There were no blackboards or bulletin boards, and very little paper, which was expensive and not always available. Students used quill pens dipped in ink to practice their penmanship and copy their lessons. They also used slate pencils, and later, pieces of chalk for writing on framed slate tablets.

The length of the school day depended on the time of year. In Salem, Massachusetts, in 1700, the school day was 7:00 a.m. to 5:00 p.m. from March 1 to November 1. When the daylight hours grew shorter—from November 1 to March 1—school began at 8:00 a.m. and ended at 4:00 p.m. There were no classes on Thanksgiving or on Wednesday and Saturday afternoons. On Sunday, everyone had to attend church services in the morning and the afternoon.

SCHOOLMASTERS

"Wanted Immediately: A Sober diligent Schoolmaster capable of teaching READING, WRITING, ARITHMETICK, and the Latin TONGUE ... Any Person qualified as above, and well recommended, will be put into immediate Possession of the School, on applying to the Minister of Charles Parish, York County."

—*The Virginia Gazette,* August 20, 1772

In the colonial era, a commonly used term for a teacher was "schoolmaster." Most were men, except for dame school teachers. For schoolmasters who had studied in a college or university, teaching was a temporary occupation on their way to a career in law or the church. But in many schools, especially those in the countryside, schoolmasters could be indentured servants, older boys, farmers, even innkeepers.

For the most part, teachers were underpaid. Even in towns with publicly funded schools, teachers' salaries were still low and partly dependent on what parents could pay as tuition. Early colonial economies relied chiefly on the **bartering** system in which products were exchanged instead of money. In a cash-poor economy, parents often paid their children's tuition with goods such as firewood, animal pelts, corn, wheat, or other agricultural products.

Some towns expected schoolmasters to take on a second job in addition to their teaching responsibilities. They might have rang the church bell on Sunday mornings, read from the Bible during church service, led the church choir, or even served as the official town gravedigger.

CORRECTIVE MEASURES

In the classroom, schoolmasters sometimes enforced discipline with a wooden cane. In private homes, a tutor or governess might use other forms of physical punishment to control students. One method was to place a "whispering stick" in the mouth of a talkative child. Secured with a strip of cloth, the stick kept the child from talking. Tutors or schoolmasters might also place a dunce cap on the head of a child who wasn't doing well in class. Dunce caps were tall, cone-shaped hats made of paper or birch bark. To be called a dunce was a humiliating insult since it meant you weren't learning fast enough to please the schoolmaster.

PRINTED MATERIALS

Learning in a colonial classroom took place in a logical sequence of stages based on the English model of literacy education. The first stage was reading. The next stage was writing. The final stage was **ciphering** (the commonly used term for arithmetic). Schoolmasters used specific types of teaching materials for each stage in the learning process, beginning with the hornbook, moving on to *The New England Primer,* and advancing to more challenging religious texts.

The use of hornbooks goes back at least as far as the fifteenth century in Europe. In colonial America, hornbooks introduced children to reading. Hornbooks were not really books. They were small paddles usually made of wood with a handle. A piece of rope passed through a hole in the handle allowed a child to hang the hornbook around his neck or from his belt.

The first hornbooks were mainly used to teach the alphabet; later versions included syllables as well as brief passages from the Bible. Colonial children learned to read using the alphabet method, which requires children to match the shapes of letters with their names. (In the phonic method, by contrast, learners match the shapes of letters with their sounds.) Instead of printing the letters, children pronounced the names of the letters out loud as a way to remember them. From individual letters, they learned to recognize syllables, then words, and finally sentences—first by spelling and then by speaking each part of a word or sentence.

The front of the hornbook contained a single piece of paper on which the letters of the alphabet, pairs of consonants and vowels, and a Christian prayer were printed. A transparent sheet of horn covered the paper and protected it from damage. Actual cow or oxen horns were used in the making of hornbooks. Craftsmen separated the outer part of the horn from the underlying bony material. They then worked the outer part until it was flat and soft enough to shape.

Not all hornbooks were made of wood. Expensive ones were made of metal, silver, pewter, or ivory. Some were edible. These were typically made of ginger-bread, which served as an incentive to reading. Children could eat their ABCs once they had learned to read them.

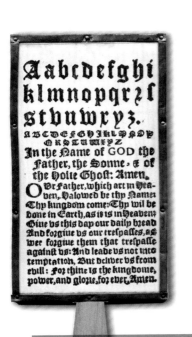

Hornbooks typically included the Lord's Prayer, the alphabet, and vowel-consonant combinations.

The word "primer" originally referred to a book of prayers. As educational tools, primers were intended to give spiritual guidance to children. They were real books with seventy or more pages. The colonies began importing primers from England around 1655.

The first completely American primer, designed and printed in Boston, was *The New England Primer*. Making its debut in the late 1680s, it was also one of the first textbooks published in colonial America. *The New England Primer* had more than 100 editions and sold between six and eight million copies. Its typical size was only two and one half-inches by four inches (6.3 by 10.1 centimeters)—mainly to save paper. It was in regular use for about 150 years. In early New England, copies of the *Primer* were available in most general stores and bookshops.

The earliest editions of this book strongly reflected the religious views of the time. Throughout its history, *The New England Primer* provided moral instruction in addition to building the reading skills of children. Most editions included the alphabet, lists of syllables and words, and a variety of literary **genres**: selections from the Bible, **proverbs**, prayers, poems, and moral tales. It was both a catechism and a textbook. As a catechism, it taught the basic rules or principles of Christianity; as a textbook, the *Primer* allowed students to improve their reading ability by tackling progressively more difficult material.

THE
New-England
PRIMER

Enlarged.

For the more eaſy attaining the true
Reading of ENGLISH.

To which is added,

The Aſſembly's Catechiſm.

PHILADELPHIA:

Printed and Sold by *B. Franklin*, and
D. Hall, in *Market-ſtreet*, 1764.

This edition of *The New England Primer* was
printed in Benjamin Franklin's shop. Primers
were used to teach religion and improve students'
reading skill.

CHAPTER FIVE

Education for Nonwhites

Classrooms for African American children and adults were rare in the colonies.

Some view our sable race with scornful eye,
"Their color is a diabolic dye."
Remember, Christians, Negroes black as Cain,
May be refin'd, and join th' angelic train.
—Phyllis Wheatley, "On Being Brought From Africa to America,"
1768

The land to which British colonists came, beginning in the early 1600s, was only a "New World" to them. For the hundreds of thousands of Native Americans living there, it was the land of their ancestors.

The first settlers may have thought the land was theirs for the taking, but they would soon discover the original inhabitants felt otherwise. In many parts of British America, encounters between indigenous people and whites led to conflict. Too often these conflicts escalated into war. Of course, relations between the two groups were not always hostile. Many well-intentioned colonial leaders attempted to foster a positive relationship with their Native American neighbors and to provide them with an education.

EFFORTS AT CONVERSION

In far too many cases, however, these efforts were part of a larger plan—to convert the Native population to Christianity. This was especially true in New England, where Puritan church leaders dreamed of creating a Christian **utopia** in which everyone, including the indigenous people, shared the same religious

beliefs. In order for Native Americans to participate in such an ideal world, Puritans would need to teach them how to read and understand English.

Throughout the colonies, Christian missionaries who reached out to Native people for the purpose of converting them typically had little or no respect for Native cultures. They regarded Native traditions and beliefs as uncivilized. For these missionaries, education would be the means to civilize the indigenous people. Once they were properly civilized, Native Americans would more likely accept the Christian faith.

John Eliot, a Puritan minister, was known as the Apostle to the Indians and translated the Bible into Algonquin.

Most Native Americans resisted attempts to become part of Christian society. They understood the need to protect and preserve their ways of life. Those relatively few who chose to give up the old ways often found themselves lost between two worlds. On the one hand, they had learned to reject their own culture. On the other hand, white society would never accept them as equals no matter how well they spoke English or how much they acted, dressed, and lived like white people.

Some Native Americans used their literacy on behalf of their own people. And some culturally sensitive white men and women helped tribes transcribe their spoken language into a written language. The ability to write in their tribal language was an important tool for preserving their culture.

In the Middle Atlantic Colonies, some missionaries incorporated indigenous languages into their teaching. This bilingual approach to literacy education allowed children to learn English without sacrificing their identity. It also enabled them to get along in white society while maintaining a strong connection with their own culture.

How successful were these literacy programs? "Only to the extent that many of the better-educated Indians used their advanced literary skills to act as cultural intermediaries between the Indian and American colonial worlds . . . Literacy empowered these individuals to at times become political, religious, and economic brokers between two rapidly changing worlds often in conflict."

African Americans

"Mr. Nath Pigott intends to open a School on Monday, next, for the Instruction of Negro's in Reading, Catechizing & Writing if required. If any are so well inclined as to send their Servants to said school near Mr. Checkley's Meeting House, care will be taken for their Instruction as aforesaid."

This advertisement for a new school in Boston was published in the April 8, 1728, edition of the *New England Weekly Journal*. Around the time of its appearance, African Americans made up only 3 percent of the population of the New England Colonies. Largely guided by their religious values, the Puritans of

Cotton Mather, like John Eliot, was a Puritan minister. Both men were committed to providing literacy education to Native Americans and African Americans.

Phillis Wheatley: Prominent Poet

Phillis Wheatley was the first African American, the first slave, and only the third woman to publish a book of poems in colonial America. Born in Seneca in West Africa, Wheatley was captured by slave traders and brought to Boston in 1761 when she was only seven or eight. Susanna Wheatley, the wife of John Wheatley, a successful Boston tailor, purchased her to be a household servant. The Wheatleys named her "Phillis" after the slave ship that brought her to America. Tutored by their teenage daughter Mary, she learned to speak and read English in a very short time.

Phillis Wheatley published her first poem at thirteen.

Seeing how talented she was, the Wheatley family nurtured her gift for language and her love of learning. She was especially fond of writing poetry. When she was around thirteen, Wheatley published her first poem. She published her only collection of her work, *Poems on Various Subjects Religious and Moral*, in 1771 when she was seventeen or eighteen, and it brought her fame. In the company of the Wheatleys' son Nathaniel, she traveled to London, where she met several famous authors and political leaders.

A few years later, shortly before Mrs. Wheatley died Phillis Wheatley received her freedom. As a free black woman living through the American Revolution, the poet found it increasingly hard to fend for herself. Although she married John Peters, a free black who aspired to become a successful businessman, Phillis Wheatley, the once celebrated and gifted writer, drifted into poverty. Near the end of her life, she supported herself by working as a cleaning woman in a Boston establishment. Her final home was a dingy apartment in a rundown part of the city. She died on December 5, 1784.

New England promoted basic literacy for blacks, most of whom were slaves. But there was also a more profit-driven reason for educating African American "Negroes": In the growing New England economy, an educated slave would have more market value and add to the net worth of white slaveholders.

The combined influence of Puritan beliefs and economic factors contributed to a rise in basic literacy among blacks in colonial New England. Influential Puritans like John Eliot and Cotton Mather supported the establishment of literacy schools for blacks. After Eliot's death, Mather continued the work that Eliot had begun. Mather encouraged slaveholders to educate their slaves. In 1717, he opened a charity school for both blacks and Native Americans. Though the school didn't last long, other colonists, inspired by Mather's determined efforts, began their own schools, such as the one noted in the *New England Weekly Journal* advertisement.

Classrooms in colonial America were sparse, with children sitting on stools or benches.

THE TRAGIC LEGACY OF SLAVERY

Slavery has existed since the beginning of human civilization. It is an institution in which certain people are regarded as mere property that can be bought and sold and forced to live with few rights and almost no personal freedom. Between the sixteenth and nineteenth centuries, the trans-Atlantic slave trade forcibly transported over 12 million men, women, and children from parts of West Africa to seaports along the eastern coast of North America, to the islands of the Caribbean, and to Brazil in South America.

In North America, slavery didn't officially end until 1865 with ratification of the thirteenth amendment. But until that happened, Christian leaders, mainly Protestant, regarded slavery as morally legitimate. They based their defense on the Bible, using specific passages from the Old and New Testaments in which slavery is viewed as an acceptable practice. These proponents of slavery argued that Jesus Christ never condemned those who owned slaves. They pointed to the letters of St. Paul in which he fails to denounce slavery. And they quoted from the books of the Old Testament in which it appears that even God approves of slavery and would oppose those arguing for its abolition.

LITERACY SCHOOLS FOR BLACKS

Anglican missionaries also opened literacy schools for blacks in colonial America. For example, around 1704, Elias Neau began a school in New York City for about twenty-eight women and eighteen men sent by slave owners. By 1705, he had more than 100 students. They met for class at 5 p.m. on Wednesdays, Fridays, and Saturdays, and again on Sunday evenings. Most of the students were adult slaves, but a few Native Americans and whites also attended. The classroom was a second-floor room in Neau's home. Each session lasted for two or more hours and focused on religious instruction. After sunset, when there wasn't enough reading light, Neau lit candles.

Fear kept Southerners from educating African Americans; this classroom shows freed slaves learning from a white school teacher in Vicksburg, Mississippi, after the Civil War.

In 1712, a group of slaves rose up against their masters. Slave owners accused Neau of training his black students to become "cunning and insolent" and blamed him for the uprising, which included arson and murder. But an investigation revealed that none of Neau's students had been involved in the revolt. The school was allowed to remain open under one condition: No blacks could be on the streets of New York after dark without a lantern. White masters saw this as an opportunity to block literacy education for blacks. They did this by preventing their slaves from carrying lanterns to school. The slave owners' strategy succeeded since most of Neau's students worked during the day and could only attend classes at night. Soon only a small number of African Americans were able to continue their education.

Neau belonged to the Society for the Propagation of the Gospel in Foreign Parts (SPG), the missionary branch of the Anglican Church of England. In 1727 the London-based director of the SPG sent out 10,000 letters to his American missionaries and also to slave owners. He urged them "as a religious duty to teach their slaves and domestics to read and write." SPG ministers like Neau opened literacy schools for blacks in the Rhode Island cities of Newport, Narragansett, and Providence. In some instances, schoolmasters sent by the SPG taught slave children and white children in the same class.

Religious Support

Quakers were strong opponents of slavery and played a major role in advancing literacy for blacks. Prominent Quaker leaders like John Woolman of New Jersey called for the education of all African Americans. In 1770, Philadelphia Quakers organized a free school for blacks where they could learn reading, writing, and arithmetic, as well as domestic skills like sewing and knitting.

By 1775, the beginning of the American Revolution, more than half of the population along the Eastern Seaboard lived in the Southern Colonies of Maryland, Virginia, the Carolinas, and Georgia. Overall, about 500,000 African Americans lived throughout the original thirteen colonies. The majority were Southern slaves.

Plantation owners resisted efforts to provide anything more than a basic education for their enslaved workers. One reason was fear. Slaves who learned to read would have access to documents written by people opposed to slavery. Some of these writers believed the only way for African Americans to achieve their freedom was to rebel against their masters. To prevent this from happening, many white slave owners preferred to keep their slaves illiterate so they would not be influenced by the "wrong" ideas.

Despite widespread resistance to the education of black Americans in the South, different religious denominations found ways to teach black children to read and write. Presbyterian minister Samuel Davies, like his colleagues, believed that religion and literacy should go hand in hand. Born in Virginia, he promoted the education of blacks and indigenous people as well as whites, and distributed many books donated from England.

In his sermons, Davies called upon people to treat everyone living in their households as members of one family. His words applied equally to children, slaves, and apprentices. He also encouraged "masters to provide a literacy education and religious worship for their slaves." Sadly, that was "a progressive concept that actually benefited relatively few African Americans in the colonial South."

The African American civil rights movement in the United States aimed to end racial discrimination and segregation in the South. The movement came to prominence beginning in the 1950s. But it was the continuation of a struggle that began centuries earlier.

Glossary

abacus

A counting device on which small beads are slid along horizontal rods within a frame. The abacus has been in use for centuries.

aristocracy

People who belong to the highest social class and enjoy considerable wealth and privilege.

bartering

The exchange of goods or services in place of money.

board of trustees

A governing group of appointed or elected individuals responsible for directing the policies of a private or public organization.

catechism

A type of book consisting of religious questions and answers. Students studying the catechism for their religion are expected to learn the answers and be able to repeat them word for word.

charity schools

Schools originated in England in the early eighteenth century as a way to provide free education to poor children. Charity schools were usually funded by private donations and run by churches. In colonial America, different religious denominations began their own charity schools.

charter

An official document issued by a government that grants an organization the right to operate.

ciphering

Another name for arithmetic.

Congregationalists

Christians who belong to the Congregational Church, a Protestant denomination that begin in the late 1500s in England. The Pilgrims in 1620 were the first Congregationalists to come to America. Also called Separatists, they advocated complete separation from the Church of England.

endowment

An amount of money or property freely given to an institution as a source of continuing financial support.

etiquette

The standards or rules for how to behave properly in social situations.

fallow

No longer seeded or used for growing crops.

genres

Types of literature or other art forms.

governesses

Female teachers employed to teach students in their home.

hornbook

Colonial school children used these small, flat wooden paddles as study aids for learning how to read. Each hornbook had a single piece of parchment paper on the front, with the letters of the alphabet written by hand. A thin covering of transparent horn, usually from a cow, kept the paper from becoming smudged or torn.

indentured

An indentured worker in colonial America was a man or woman under contract to work for a certain period of time without the right to quit the job. Apprenticeships were a form of indentured labor.

medieval

Describes a period of time in the history of Europe from around 500 CE to around 1500 CE.

missionary

A member of a religious denomination who travels to another region or country to spread his faith or to work to improve the lives of others.

nonsectarian

Having no specific connection with any religion or religious sect.

old field school

A type of school in the colonial South usually found on farmland no longer used to grow crops.

parochial

A parochial school is one that is supported and operated by a church.

philanthropist

Someone who gives large amounts of money to causes or institutions working for the good of humanity.

Pilgrims

The Pilgrims were English Separatists who sailed to New England to escape persecution and to establish a colony where they could practice their religion in freedom.

Protestant

Protestantism is one of the three major branches of Christianity. It began in the sixteenth century as an attempt to reform the Roman Catholic Church. A Protestant is someone who belongs to any of the religious denominations associated with Protestant Christianity.

proverb

A short saying that expresses a well-known truth or commonly accepted bit of wisdom such as "All that glitters is not gold." Proverbs from the Bible's Book of Proverbs were used in colonial America to teach children the values of their religions.

Puritan

Puritans belonged to a Christian movement that began in seventeenth-century England. They believed the Church of England had not gone far enough in removing the influences of Roman Catholicism. Puritans wanted a "purer" form of Protestant Christianity.

Quakers

Quakers are members of the Religious Society of Friends, a Christian denomination that began in the mid-1600s in England under the leadership of George Fox. Fox taught that each person possesses an Inner Light that can guide him or her through life.

secular

Having nothing to do with religious or spiritual matters.

sexton

Someone who takes care of a church's buildings and surrounding property.

theology

The study of religion, especially questions about the nature of God and religious truth.

utopia

An ideal society founded on principles shared by all members.

Further Reading

Nonfiction

Hinman, Bonnie. *The Scoop on School and Work in Colonial America.* North Mankato, MN: Capstone Press, 2012.

Nardo, Don. *Daily Life in Colonial America.* Detroit, MI: Lucent Books, 2010.

Roberts, Russell. *Life in Colonial America.* Hockessin, DE: Mitchell Lane Publishers, 2008.

Spotlight on America: Colonial America. Westminster, CA: Teacher Created Resources, Inc., 2010.

Wallenfeldt, Jeff, ed. *From Columbus to Colonial America: 1492 to 1763.* New York, NY: Britannica Encyclopedia Publishing in association with Rosen Educational Services, 2012.

Fiction

Cooney, Caroline B. *The Ransom of Mercy Carter.* New York, NY: Ember, 2011.

Cooper, James Fenimore. *The Last of the Mohicans.* New York, NY: Atheneum Books for Young Readers, 2013.

Lassieur, Allison. *Colonial America: An Interactive History Adventure.* North Mankato, Minnesota: Capstone Press, 2011.

Sedgwick, Catharine Maria. *Hope Leslie, or Early Times in Massachusetts.* Mineola, NY: Dover Publications, Inc., 2011.

WEBSITES

The Library of Congress: Colonial America (1492–1763).
www.americaslibrary.gov/jb/colonial/jb_colonial_subj.html
Information about America's story is provided by America's library.

Public Broadcasting Service: School: The Story of American Public Education.
www.pbs.org/kcet/publicschool/evolving_classroom/books.html
Find a wealth of information about education from the Public Broadcasting Service.

Schooling, Education, and Literacy in Colonial America.
alumni.cc.gettysburg.edu/~s330558/schooling.html
Check out this primer on colonial era educational resources and classrooms from Gettysburg College.

SELECTED BIBLIOGRAPHY

"American Education: Colonial America." oregonstate.edu/ instruct/ed416/ae1.html

American History: From Revolution to Reconstruction and Beyond. "How They Were Schooled." www.let.rug.nl/usa/outlines/history-1963/ the-colonial-period/how they-were-schooled.php

Childhood in Colonial America. "Education and Literacy." www3.gettysburg.edu/~tshannon/341/sites/Childhood/ Education%20and%20Literacy.htm

The Colonist's Journal. "Colonial Education in New England Colonies." sites.google.com/site/thecolonistsjournal/colonial-education-in-new-en- gland-colonies

Education World. "Back in the Day: Lessons from Colonial Classrooms." www.educationworld.com/a_lesson/lesson166.shtml

FAQS.org. "Education, United States: Schools in Colonial America." www.faqs.org/childhood/Co-Fa/Education-United-States.html

Gordon, Edward E., and Elaine H. Gordon. *Literacy in America: Historic Journey and Contemporary Solutions.* Westport, CT: Praeger Publishers: 2003.

Gray, Edward G. *Colonial America: A History in Documents.* New York, NY: Oxford University Press, Inc., 2003.

Grenet, Phyllis. "American Life: A Comparison of Colonial Life to Today's Life: Education." www.yale.edu/ynhti/curriculum/units/1990/5/90.05.04.x.html#c

Hinman, Bonnie. *The Scoop on School and Work in Colonial America.* North Mankato, MN: Capstone Press, 2012.

The History of Education in America. "Colonial Education: Education for Boys and Girls." www.chesapeake.edu/Library/EDU_101/eduhist_colonial.asp

Library of Congress. "Colonial Settlement (1492–1763)." www.loc.gov/teachers/additionalresources/relatedresources/ushist/chrono/colonial.html

Library of Congress, Manuscript Reading Room. "Highlight: George Washington's School Copy Books, ca. 1745–1747." www.loc.gov/rr/mss/gwcopybooks.html

Mather, Cotton. "The Education of Children." www.spurgeon.org/~phil/mather/edkids.htm

Melton, Buckner F., ed. *The Quotable Founding Fathers.* Dulles, Virginia: Potomac Books, Inc. 2005.

Monaghan, E. Jennifer. *Learning to Read and Write in Colonial America.* Amherst and Boston: University of Massachusetts Press: 2005.

National Women's History Museum. "The History of Women and Education." www.nwhm.org/online-exhibits/education/1700s_1. htm

The New England Primer Index. "The New England Primer." www.sacred-texts.com/chr/nep

Putnam, Eleanor. "A Salem Dame-School." *Atlantic Monthly,* January 1885. digital.library.cornell.edu/cgi/t/text/pageviewer-idx?c=atla;cc=atla;rgn=full%20text;idno=atla0055-1;didno=atla0055-1;view=image;seq=00059;node=atla0055-1:1

Sateren, Shelley Swanson. *Going to School in Colonial America.* Mankato, MN: Capstone Press, 2002.

"Schooling, Education, and Literacy in Colonial America." alumni.cc.gettysburg.edu/~s330558/schooling.html

Taylor, Alan. *American Colonies.* New York, NY: Viking Penguin, 2001.

Wallenfeldt, Jeff, ed. *From Columbus to Colonial America: 1492 to 1763.* New York, NY: Britannica Educational Publishing in association with Rosen Educational Services, 2012.

Wilmore, Kathy. *A Day in the Life of a Colonial Schoolteacher.* New York, NY: Rosen Publishing Group, Inc., 2000.

Quotation Sources

CHAPTER 1: EDUCATION IN THE COLONIES

p. 13, Gordon, Edward E., and Elaine H. Gordon. *Literacy in America: Historic Journey and Contemporary Solutions* (Westport, CT: Praeger Publishers: 2003) p. 40.

p. 14, Gordon. *Literacy in America: Historic Journey and Contemporary Solutions*, p. 41.

p. 15, www.sidwell.edu/about-sfs/quaker-values/testimonies/that-of-god-in-everyone/index.aspx

p. 15, Gordon, *Literacy in America*, p. 46.

p. 16, Project Gutenberg, "Journal & Letters of Philip Vickers Fithian, 1773–1774," www.gutenberg.org/files/40044/40044-h/40044-h.htm

p. 18, Project Gutenberg, "Journal & Letters of Philip Vickers Fithian, 1773–1774," www.gutenberg.org/files/40044/40044-h/40044-h.htm

p. 21, Gordon, *Literacy in America*, p. 68.

p. 22, *Foundations Magazine*, "George Washington's Rules of Civility & Decent Behaviour In Company and Conversation," www.foundationsmag.com/civility.html

CHAPTER 2: TYPES OF SCHOOLING

p. 29, Sheldon, George. *A History of Deerfield, Massachusetts*, pp. 243–244, books.google.com/books?id=W2wWAAAAYAAJ&pg=PA243&lpg=PA243&dq=Mrs.+Hannah+Beaman+Indian+attack+deerfield&source=bl&ots=DK3x6VR9-9&sig=uH9RjvRY0aCKU5diW7fpc5ZC-

joU&hl=en&sa=X&ei=ViiyUsrfMOq0sQSE04DYAQ&ved=0C-
DEQ6AEwAQ#v=onepage&q=Mrs.%20Hannah%20Beaman%20
Indian%20attack%20deerfield&f=false

p. 32, Washington State Department of Labor & Industries. "History of
Apprenticeship," www.lni.wa.gov/TradesLicensing/Apprenticeship/
About/History

p. 34, Washington State Department of Labor & Industries. "History of
Apprenticeship," www.lni.wa.gov/TradesLicensing/Apprenticeship/
About/History

CHAPTER 3: COLLEGES IN COLONIAL AMERICA

p. 41, William & Mary, "History & Traditions,"
www.wm.edu/about/history/index.php

p. 41, Yale University, "History," www.yale.edu/about/history.html

p. 43, www.princeton.edu/main/about/history/glance

p. 45, www.archives.upenn.edu/histy/genlhistory/brief.html

CHAPTER 4: THE COLONIAL CLASSROOM

p. 50, Burton, Warren, "Lesson Plans/Sturbridge Village," excerpt from
The District School As It Was, resources.osv.org/school/lesson_plans/
ShowLessons.php?PageID=P&LessonID=30&DocID=95&UnitID=

p. 52, PBS.org, "Only a Teacher: Teaching Timeline, 1772 to Late 18th
Century," www.pbs.org/onlyateacher/timeline.html

CHAPTER 5: EDUCATION FOR NONWHITES

p. 60, Gordon, *Literacy in America*, p. 203.

p. 66, Ibid., p. 228.

Index

Page numbers in **boldface** are images.

Native Americans, 17, **17**, 38, 41,
    46, 47, 57–60, **60**, 62–63
Neau, Elias, 63, 66
nonsectarian, 45

old field school, 21–23, 26,

parochial, 13, 16, 26
philanthropist, 41
Pilgrims, 9
Protestant, 5, 13–14, 37, 42, 63
proverb, 54
Puritan, 5, 9–11, 13, 34–35, 37–38,
    57–58, **59**, 60, **60**, 62

Quakers, 5, 16–18, 66

schooling
    apprenticeship, 6, 11, 18, 25–26,
        29, 33–34
    dame, 29–30, 51
    Latin grammar, 17, 21, 30–31,
        33, 46–47
    See also, old field schools

secular, 11, 47
sexton, 23

theology, 20

utopia, 57

Wheatley, Phillis, 57, 61, **61**
Woolman, John, **17**, 66

Author Biography

George Capaccio has been a poet, artist educator, and writer. A native New Englander, he graduated from the University of Massachusetts with a bachelor of arts degree in English literature. Since he began writing for children and older students, he's written fiction and nonfiction on a variety of topics—the sun and the planets, the nervous system, America's historic highways, and even what life was like during the Middle Ages.

For many years, Capaccio worked in Boston public schools as an artist educator. In this role he created and implemented curriculum enrichment programs for K–8 students. His primary responsibility was to help build the literacy skills of his students through storytelling and creative drama. His experience working in multicultural classrooms was an invaluable asset in the writing of this book. In particular, it enabled him to better appreciate the challenges facing colonial-era children in their efforts to become literate.